Thoughts of You

Thoughts of You

Published by Garborg's Heart 'n Home, Inc.
P. O. Box 20132, Bloomington, MN 55420

Photography copyright © by Virginia Dixon
Design by Mick Thurber

SPCN 5-5044-0292-1

Happiness is found along the way, not at the end of the road.

God never abandons anyone on whom He has set His love; nor does Christ the Good Shepherd ever lose track of His sheep.

J. I. PACKER

JULY 3

No good thing will he withhold from those who walk along his paths.

PSALM 84:11   TLB

JUNE 30

Each day brings us a chance to do better and to make good. It is as though our slate has had the smudges of yesterday wiped out.

L. BEVAN JONES

Everything God does is love—even when we do not understand Him.

BASILEA SCHLINK

*A friend is a gift
whose worth cannot
be measured except
by the heart.*

See Jesus in
everything and in
everything you will
find blessing.

Be full of sympathy toward each other, loving one another with tender hearts and humble minds.

1 PETER 3:8 TLB

I believe in the sun even when it is not shining, in love even when I am alone, and in God even when He is silent.

JUNE 27

When we are in a situation where Jesus is all we have, we soon discover He is all we really need.

GIGI GRAHAM TCHIVIDJIAN

JULY 7

*Lift up your eyes.
Your heavenly Father waits
to bless you—in inconceivable
ways to make your life what
you never dreamed it could be.*

JANETTE OKE

*Life is the first gift,
love is the second, and
understanding the third.*

MARGE PIERCY

Do not worry about your life.... Look at the birds of the air; they do not sow or reap or store away in barns, and yet your heavenly Father feeds them. Are you not much more valuable than they?

MATTHEW 6:25,26 NIV

Reach high, for stars lie hidden in your soul. Dream deep, for every dream precedes the goal.

PAMELA VAULL STARR

JULY 9

We are of such value to God that He...will go to any length to seek us, even to being lifted high upon a cross to draw us back to himself. We can only respond by loving God for His love.

CATHERINE OF SIENA

If there is anything better than being loved, it is loving.

JULY 10

You made us for yourself, O God, and our hearts are restless until they rest in You.

AUGUSTINE

JUNE 23

The beauty that is seen is partly within those who see it.

Each dawn holds a new hope for a new plan, making the start of each day the start of a new life.

GINA BLAIR

JUNE 22

Live your life while you have it. Life is a splendid gift—there is nothing small about it.

FLORENCE NIGHTINGALE

JULY 12

The best things are nearest: breath in your nostrils, light in your eyes, flowers at your feet, duties at your hand, the path of God just before you.

ROBERT LOUIS STEVENSON

To love someone is
to seek his or her best
and highest good.

We fix our eyes not on what is seen, but on what is unseen. For what is seen is temporary, but what is unseen is eternal.

2 CORINTHIANS 4:18 NIV

JUNE 20

*Love comes out
of heaven unasked
and unsought.*

PEARL S. BUCK

Love is the highest gift of God; humble, gentle, patient love.

JOHN WESLEY

*Friendship is precious,
not only in the shade, but in
the sunshine of life; and thanks
to a benevolent arrangement
of things, the greater part
of life is sunshine.*

THOMAS JEFFERSON

*Delight yourself
in the surprises
of today.*

To love someone means to see him as God intended him.

FEODOR DOSTOEVSKY

JULY 16

Always laugh when you can; it is cheap medicine. Merriment is...the sunny side of existence.

LORD BYRON

The one thing worth living for is to keep one's soul pure.

MARCUS AURELIUS

JULY 17

Think of it! We are loved eternally, totally, individually, unreservedly! Nothing can take God's love away.

GLORIA GAITHER

JUNE 16

My children, we should love people not only with words and talk, but by our actions and true caring.

1 JOHN 3:18 NCV

JULY 18

A joyful heart is like a sunshine of God's love.

MOTHER TERESA

*Happiness is my
friend's hand.*

GILLIAN QUEEN, AGE 10

JULY 19

*Know that you
yourself are a
miracle.*

NORMAN VINCENT PEALE

JUNE 14

There is no surprise more magical than the surprise of being loved. It is the finger of God on [our] shoulder.

MARGARET KENNEDY

Light tomorrow with today!

ELIZABETH BARRETT BROWNING

*Hold fast your dreams!
Within your heart keep
one still, secret spot
where dreams may go
and, sheltered so, may
thrive and grow.*

DRISCOLL

We've missed the full impact of God's love if we have not discovered what it is to be ourselves, irreplaceable in His sight, unique among all others.

JUNE 12

Nobody has ever measured, even poets, how much a heart can hold.

ZELDA FITZGERALD

May the Lord bless and protect you; may the Lord's face radiate with joy because of you; may he be gracious to you, show you his favor, and give you his peace.

NUMBERS 6:24-26 TLB

JUNE 11

May God send His love like sunshine in His warm and gentle way, to fill each corner of your heart each moment of today.

*Joy is the echo
of God's life
within us.*

JOSEPH MARMION

JUNE 10

Friendship is sharing openly, laughing often, trusting always, caring deeply.

The hand that gives,
gathers.

ENGLISH PROVERB

Everything God created is good.

1 TIMOTHY 4:4 NIV

He made you so you could share in His creation, could love and laugh and know Him person to person.

TED GRIFFEN

Graciously, God leaves all my mistakes where the sea meets the horizon—forgotten forever in infinity.

JULY 26

Lovely, complicated
wrappings
Sheath the gift of
one day more;
Breathless, I untie
the package—
Never lived this day before!

GLORIA GAITHER

JUNE 7

God is the sunshine that warms us, the rain that melts the frost and waters the young plants. The presence of God is a climate of strong and bracing love, always there.

JOAN ARNOLD

JULY 27

In the deepest heart of every person, God planted a longing for himself, as He is: a God of love.

EUGENIA PRICE

JUNE 6

The sun does not shine for a few trees and flowers, but for the wide world's joy.

HENRY WARD BEECHER

JULY 28

All the things in this world are gifts and signs of God's love to us. The whole world is a love letter from God.

PETER KREEFT

Hope is faith holding out its hands in the dark.

GEORGE ILES

JULY 29

You give [us] drink from your river of delights. For with you is the fountain of life; in your light we see light.

PSALM 36:8,9 NIV

JUNE 4

You're blessed when you feel you've lost what is most dear to you. Only then can you be embraced by the One most dear to you.

MATTHEW 5:4 TM

JULY 30

The goodness of God is infinitely more wonderful than we will ever be able to comprehend.

A. W. TOZER

Flowers leave their fragrance on the hand that bestows them.

CHINESE PROVERB

Keep your heart clean and bright; you are the window through which others may see God.

When we call on God, He bends down His ear to listen, as a father bends down to listen to his little child.

ELIZABETH CHARLES

We have been in God's thought from all eternity, and in His creative love, His attention never leaves us.

MICHAEL QUOIST

JUNE 1

*Love is the seed
of all hope. It is the
enticement to trust, to
risk, to try, to go on.*

GLORIA GAITHER

AUGUST 2

The Lord will work out his plans for my life — for your lovingkindness, Lord, continues forever.

PSALM 138:8   TLB

All that is worth cherishing begins in the heart.

SUZANNE CHAPIN

God's promise of
love and life everlasting
reaches far beyond
the scope of my
imagination.

MAY 30

Because the Lord is my Shepherd, I have everything I need! He lets me rest in meadow grass and leads me beside the quiet streams. He gives me new strength. He helps me do what honors him the most.

PSALM 23:1-3 TLB

AUGUST 4

You have a unique message to deliver, a unique song to sing, a unique act of love to bestow. This message, this song, and this act of love have been entrusted exclusively to the one and only you.

JOHN POWELL, S. J.

MAY 29

If we just give God the little that we have, we can trust Him to make it go around.

GLORIA GAITHER

AUGUST 5

The Lord's goodness surrounds us at every moment. I walk through it almost with difficulty, as through thick grass and flowers.

R. W. BARBER

MAY 28

Friendship is something that raised us almost above humanity.... It is the sort of love one can imagine between angels.

C. S. LEWIS

He meets us as we are; He loves us too much to leave us as we've been.

MAY 27

The best and most beautiful things in the world cannot be seen or even touched. They must be felt with the heart.

HELEN KELLER

The Lord who created you says... I have called you by name; you are mine.

ISAIAH 43:1 TLB

MAY 26

*God makes our lives
a medley of joy and
tears, hope and help,
love and encouragement.*

When I walk by the wayside, He is along with me.... Amid all my forgetfulness of Him, He never forgets me.

THOMAS CHALMERS

MAY 25

No wonder we are happy in the Lord! For we are trusting him. We trust his holy name. Yes, Lord, let your constant love surround us, for our hopes are in you alone.

PSALM 33:21,22 TLB

AUGUST 9

If you have a special need, focus your full attention on the goodness and greatness of your father rather than on the size of your need. Your need is so small compared to His ability to meet it.

MAY 24

A friend is one to whom one may pour out all the contents of one's heart—chaff and grain together—knowing that gentle hands will take and sift it, keep what is worth keeping, and with a breath of kindness, blow the rest away.

GEORGE ELIOT

We need time to dream, time to remember, time to reach the infinite. Time to be.

GLADYS TABER

Pleasure is very seldom found where it is sought. Our brightest blazes are commonly kindled by unexpected sparks.

SAMUEL JOHNSON

Time has a wonderful way of showing us what really matters.

Faith is not
believing that God
can—it's knowing
that He will.

AUGUST 12

I will not forget you. See, I have inscribed you on the palms of my hands.

ISAIAH 49:15,16   NRSV

MAY 21

The joy that you give to others is the joy that comes back to you.

JOHN GREENLEAF WHITTIER

The gift of happiness belongs to those who unwrap it.

MAY 20

Be kind to one another, tenderhearted, forgiving one another, as God in Christ has forgiven you.

EPHESIANS 4:32 NRSV

AUGUST 14

You will find, as you look back upon your life, that the moments when you have really lived are the moments when you have done things in the spirit of love.

HENRY DRUMMOND

MAY 19

There are moments when our hearts nearly burst within us for the sheer joy of being alive.... The warmth of another's eyes, the fresh scent of rain on a hot summer's eve—moments like these renew in us a heartfelt appreciation for life.

GWEN WEISING

One of life's greatest treasures is the love that binds hearts together in friendship.

MAY 18

When you're with someone you trust in, never needing to pretend, Someone who helps you know yourself... you know you're with a friend.

AMANDA BRADLEY

AUGUST 16

Happiness is a perfume you cannot pour on others without getting a few drops on yourself.

RALPH WALDO EMERSON

Friendships begun in this world can be taken up again in heaven, never to be broken off.

FRANCIS DE SALES

I have loved you with an everlasting love; I have drawn you with loving-kindness.

JEREMIAH 31:3   NIV

Of all best things upon the earth, a faithful friend is the best.

God's peace is joy resting. His joy is peace dancing.

F. F. BRUCE

Your goodness and unfailing kindness shall be with me all of my life, and afterwards I will live with you forever in your home.

PSALM 23:6 TLB

AUGUST 19

We think God's love rises and falls with our performance. It doesn't.... He loves you for whose you are: you are His child.

MAX LUCADO

MAY 14

We have not made ourselves; we are the gift of the living God to one another.

REINE DUELL BETHANY

AUGUST 20

*God's love is like a
river springing up...flowing
endlessly through His creation,
filling all things with life
and goodness and strength.*

THOMAS MERTON

*Together is
the nicest place
to be.*

AUGUST 21

You are God's created beauty and the focus of His affection and delight.

JANET L. WEAVER

MAY 12

The things that matter the most in this world, they can never be held in our hand.

GLORIA GAITHER

AUGUST 22

*Surely I am
with you always,
to the very end
of the age.*

MATTHEW 28:20 NIV

MAY 11

Faith makes all things possible. Hope makes all things bright. Love makes all things easy.

God knows the rhythm of my spirit and knows my heart thoughts. He is as close as breathing.

See to it that you really do love each other warmly, with all your hearts.

1 PETER 1:22 TLB

AUGUST 24

Pay attention to the small things—the kite flies because of its tail.

HAWAIIAN PROVERB

MAY 9

Our road will be smooth
and untroubled
no matter what care
life may send;
If we travel the pathway
together,
and walk side by side
with a friend.

AUGUST 25

I don't know what the future holds, but I know who holds the future.

SAMUEL JOHNSON

I am beginning to learn that it is the sweet, simple things of life which are the real ones after all.

LAURA INGALLS WILDER

AUGUST 26

*The mercy of our God
is very tender, and heaven's
dawn is about to break
upon us, to give light...
and to guide us to the
path of peace.*

LUKE 1:78,79   TLB

MAY 7

Where your pleasure is, there is your treasure; where your treasure, there your heart; where your heart, there your happiness.

AUGUSTINE

Somewhere on the great world the sun is always shining, and just so sure as you live, it will sometime shine on you. The dear God made it so. There is so much sunshine we must all have our share.

MYRTLE REED

MAY 6

To love a person is to learn the song that is in their heart, and to sing it to them when they have forgotten.

Every time I begin to feel that there just isn't any more strength in me, I end up knowing that there is more...in Him.

GLORIA GAITHER

MAY 5

If you love someone you will be loyal to him no matter what the cost.

1 CORINTHIANS 13:7 TLB

AUGUST 29

God...knows our needs. He anticipates our crises. He is moved by our weaknesses. He stands ready to come to our rescue. And at just the right moment He steps in.

CHARLES R. SWINDOLL

MAY 4

*It is not how much
we have, but how much
we enjoy, that makes
happiness.*

CHARLES H. SPURGEON

AUGUST 30

What a wonderful God we have—he is the father of our Lord Jesus Christ, the source of every mercy, and the one who so wonderfully comforts and strengthens us.

2 CORINTHIANS 1:3,4 TLB

MAY 3

We can make up our minds whether our lives in this world shall…be beautiful and fragrant like the lilies of the field.

FATHER ANDREW SDC

[God] will never
let you be shaken or
moved from your place
near His heart.

JONI EARECKSON TADA

Far away, there in the sunshine, are my highest aspirations. I may not reach them but I can look up and see their beauty, believe in them, and try to follow where they lead.

LOUISA MAY ALCOTT

Today a new sun rises for me; everything lives, everything is animated, everything seems to speak to me of my passion, everything invites me to cherish it.

ANNE DE LENCLOS

MAY 1

The Lord searches every heart and understands every motive behind the thoughts. If you seek him, he will be found by you.

1 CHRONICLES 28:9 NIV

*May you be
ever present in
the garden of
His love.*

Every moment is full of wonder, and God is always present.

SEPTEMBER 3

The Lord loves the just and will not forsake his faithful ones. They will be protected forever.

PSALM 37:28 NIV

It's the little things that make up the richest part of the tapestry of our lives.

Live near to God, and all things will appear to you little in comparison with eternal realities.

MCCHEYNE

APRIL 28

Everyone was meant to share
God's all-abiding love and care;
He saw that we would need
to know
a way to let these feelings
show....
So God made hugs.

JILL WOLF

SEPTEMBER 5

The uncertainties of the present always give way to the enchanted possibilities of the future.

KIRKLAND

APRIL 27

Jesus Christ opens wide the doors of the treasure house of God's promises, and bids us go in and take with boldness the riches that are ours.

CORRIE TEN BOOM

Before me, even as behind, God is—and all is well.

JOHN GREENLEAF WHITTIER

APRIL 26

Seek the Lord your God, you will find him if you seek him with all your heart and with all your soul.

DEUTERONOMY 4:29 NIV

It is only with the heart that one can see rightly.

ANTOINE DE SAINT-EXUPÉRY

APRIL 25

To love and to be loved is the greatest happiness of existence.

SYDNEY SMITH

He surrounds me with lovingkindness and tender mercies. He fills my life with good things.

PSALM 103:4,5 TLB

Our happiness is greatest when we contribute most to the happiness of others.

HARRIET SHEPARD

You are God's created beauty and the focus of His affection and delight.

JANET L. WEAVER

*Lord, give me an open
heart to find you everywhere,
to glimpse the heaven enfolded
in a bud, and to experience
eternity in the smallest act
of love.*

MOTHER TERESA

SEPTEMBER 10

*Knowing what to say
is not always necessary;
just the presence of a caring
friend can make a world
of difference.*

SHERI CURRY

APRIL 22

God's forgiveness and love exist for you as if you were the only person on earth.

CECIL OSBORNE

Favorite people, favorite places, favorite memories of the past... these are the joys of a lifetime...these are the things that last.

APRIL 21

As you know him better, he will give you...everything you need for living a truly good life: he even shares his own glory and his own goodness with us!

2 PETER 1:3 TLB

Having someone who understands is a great blessing for ourselves. Being someone who understands is a great blessing to others.

JANETTE OKE

APRIL 20

*I marvel at the way
that hope keeps
breaking through;
It is the Life in me
that keeps on reenacting
resurrection.*

GLORIA GAITHER

SEPTEMBER 13

*When we obey him,
every path he guides us
on is fragrant with
his lovingkindness
and his truth.*

PSALM 25:10 TLB

The good for which
we are born into this
world is that we may
learn to love.

GEORGE MACDONALD

To love someone is to look into the face of God.

APRIL 18

God loves us; not because we are lovable but because He is love, not because He needs to receive but because He delights to give.

C. S. LEWIS

Happiness is being at peace; being with loved ones; being comfortable…. But most of all, it's having those loved ones.

JOHNNY CASH

APRIL 17

Our Lord has written the promise of the resurrection, not in books alone, but in every leaf in springtime.

MARTIN LUTHER

To the children of God
there stands, behind all that
changes and can change,
only one unchangeable joy.
That is God.

HANNAH WHITALL SMITH

APRIL 16

Oh, love me—and right now!—hold me tight! just the way you promised. Now comfort me so I can live, really live; your revelation is the tune I dance to.

PSALM 119:76,77 TM

Laughter is the shortest distance between two people.

VICTOR BORGE

To love for the sake
of being loved is human,
But to love for the sake
of loving is angelic.

DE LAMARTINE

SEPTEMBER 18

Love allows us to live and through living we grow in loving.

EVELYN MANDEL

APRIL 14

*Line by line, moment
by moment, special times
are etched into our memories
in the permanent ink of
everlasting love in our
relationships.*

GLORIA GAITHER

SEPTEMBER 19

My help comes from the Lord, who made heaven and earth. He...will neither slumber nor sleep. The Lord is your keeper; the Lord is your shade at your right hand.

PSALM 121:2-5 NRSV

The great Easter truth is not that we are to live newly after death, but that we are to be new here and now by the power of the resurrection.

PHILLIPS BROOKS

Joy is a light that fills you with hope and faith and love.

ADELA ROGERS ST. JOHNS

Love has its source in God, for love is the very essence of His being.

KAY ARTHUR

Few delights can equal the mere presence of one whom we trust utterly.

GEORGE MACDONALD

APRIL 11

The only thing that counts is faith expressing itself through love.

GALATIANS 5:6 NIV

SEPTEMBER 22

The supreme happiness of life is the conviction that we are loved.

VICTOR HUGO

*Jesus cannot forget
us; we have been
graven on the palms
of His hands.*

LOIS PICILLO

When I realize how great God is, my problems become so small. There's no reason to worry anymore.

CECE WINANS

APRIL 9

As Jesus stepped into the garden, you were in His prayers. As Jesus looked into heaven, you were in His vision.... His final prayer was about you. His final pain was for you. His final passion was you.

MAX LUCADO

SEPTEMBER 24

The steadfast love of the Lord never ceases, his mercies never come to an end; they are new every morning; great is your faithfulness.

LAMENTATIONS 3:22,23 NRSV

Love is a great thing. By itself it makes everything that is heavy light; and it smoothes every rough place.

Whenever I think of you, I smile inside.

Being with you is like walking on a very clear morning— definitely the sensation of belonging there.

E. B. WHITE

Go outside, to the fields, enjoy nature and the sunshine, go out and try to recapture happiness in yourself and in God. Think of all the beauty that's still left in and around you and be happy!

ANNE FRANK

[Jesus] became what we are that He might make us what He is.

ATHANASIUS

People need joy;
quite as much
as clothing.

MARGRET COLLIER GRAHAM

APRIL 5

He will keep in perfect peace all those who trust in him, whose thoughts turn often to the Lord! Trust in the Lord God always.

ISAIAH 26:3,4   TLB

SEPTEMBER 28

Love doesn't make the world go round. Love is what makes the ride worthwhile.

FRANKLIN P. JONES

APRIL 4

When you feel in your own heart the suffering of Christ, remember the resurrection has to come, the joy of Easter has to dawn.

MOTHER TERESA

SEPTEMBER 29

I am still confident of this: I will see the goodness of the Lord in the land of the living. Wait for the Lord; be strong and take heart and wait for the Lord.

PSALM 27:13,14 NIV

Christ is the still point of the turning world.

T. S. ELIOT

SEPTEMBER 30

Sorrows come to stretch out spaces in the heart for joy.

EDWIN MARKHAM

APRIL 2

To love is to receive
a glimpse of heaven.

Let love be your
greatest aim.

1 CORINTHIANS 14:1   TLB

The truly happy people are those who have a source of happiness too deep to be seriously disturbed by ordinary troubles.

MARION K. RICH

APRIL 1

God not only knows us, but He values us highly in spite of all He knows.... We are made in His image and He sacrificed His Son that each one of us might be one with Him. Sparrows are sold at two for a penny; we were bought with a much higher price.

JOHN FISCHER

Love is a fruit in season at all times and within the reach of every hand.

MOTHER TERESA

MARCH 31

Love knows no limit to
its endurance, no end to its
trust, no fading of its hope;
it can outlast anything.
Love never fails.

1 CORINTHIANS 13:7,8 PHILLIPS

OCTOBER 3

*May you be given
more and more of
God's kindness, peace,
and love.*

JUDE 1:2 TLB

MARCH 30

*Herein is joy,
amid the ebb and
flow of the passing
world: our God remains
unmoved, and His throne
endures forever.*

ROBERT COLEMAN

Happiness is inward and not outward; and so it does not depend on what we have, but on what we are.

HENRY VAN DYKE

Where Jesus has passed by...He leaves behind a trail of wholeness, completeness, and joy that is unmistakably "His touch."

GLORIA GAITHER

OCTOBER 5

To be grateful is to recognize the love of God in everything He has given us— and He has given us everything. Every breath we draw is a gift of His love, every moment of existence, a gift of grace.

THOMAS MERTON

*Every single act
of love bears the
imprint of God.*

OCTOBER 6

God is in His heaven—all is right with the world!

ROBERT BROWNING

MARCH 27

Trust God where you cannot trace Him. Do not try to penetrate the cloud He brings over you; rather look to the bow that is on it. The mystery is God's; the promise is yours.

JOHN MACDUFF

OCTOBER 7

What the heart gives away is never gone.... It is kept in the heart of others.

ROBIN ST. JOHN

*Love is a good
above all others;
love alone makes
every burden light.*

OCTOBER 8

For the soul of every living thing is in the hand of God, and the breath of all mankind.

JOB 12:10 TLB

MARCH 25

Your heavenly father knows your needs. He will always give you all you need from day to day.

LUKE 12:30,31 TLB

*The God who created...
pays attention to very big
things and to very small ones.
What matters to me matters
to Him, and that changes
my life.*

ELISABETH ELLIOT

The soul can split
the sky in two, and
let the face of God
shine through.

EDNA ST. VINCENT MILLAY

OCTOBER 10

This day is all that is good and fair. It is too dear, with its hopes and invitations, to waste a moment on yesterdays.

RALPH WALDO EMERSON

The stars may fall, but God's promises will stand and be fulfilled.

J. I. PACKER

OCTOBER 11

Happiness comes of the capacity to feel deeply, to enjoy simply, to think freely, to risk life, to be needed.

STORM JAMESON

Take spring when it comes, and rejoice. Take happiness when it comes, and rejoice. Take love when it comes, and rejoice.

CARL EWALD

The value of a person...is measured in the heart and mind of God.

JOHN FISCHER

MARCH 21

To believe that God can reach us and bless us in the ordinary [events] of daily life is the stuff of prayer. You see, the only place God can bless us is right where we are, because that is the only place we are!

RICHARD FOSTER

OCTOBER 13

The love of the Father is like a sudden rain shower that will pour forth when you least expect it, catching you up into wonder and praise.

RICHARD FOSTER

MARCH 20

Love the Lord your God with all your heart and with all your soul and with all your strength.

DEUTERONOMY 6:5 NIV

The eternal God is your Refuge, and underneath are the everlasting arms.

DEUTERONOMY 33:27 TLB

Blessed is the influence of one true, loving human soul on another.

GEORGE ELIOT

OCTOBER 15

Do you believe that God is near? He wants you to. He wants you to know that He is in the midst of your world.... And He is more than near. He is active.

MAX LUCADO

MARCH 18

Have confidence in God's mercy, for when you think He is a long way from you, He is often quite near.

THOMAS À KEMPIS

Instead of a gem or even a flower, cast the gift of a lovely thought into the heart of a friend; that would be giving even as an angel gives.

GEORGE MACDONALD

MARCH 17

There is only one happiness in life, to love and to be loved.

GEORGE SAND

OCTOBER 17

Because of what Christ has done we have become gifts to God that he delights in.

EPHESIANS 1:11 TLB

MARCH 16

Every morning is a fresh opportunity to find God's extraordinary joy in the most ordinary places.

JANET L. WEAVER

*Don't be afraid.
God is for you.*

BILLY GRAHAM

MARCH 15

Every good and perfect gift is from above, coming down from the Father of the heavenly lights, who does not change like shifting shadows.

JAMES 1:17 NIV

*Every day holds
the possibility
of a miracle.*

MARCH 14

God loves us, and the will of love is always blessing for its loved ones.

HANNAH WHITALL SMITH

OCTOBER 20

*I will lie down
in peace and sleep,
for though I am alone,
O Lord, you will
keep me safe.*

PSALM 4:8 TLB

MARCH 13

*A joyful heart is
like the sunshine
of God's love.*

MOTHER TERESA

OCTOBER 21

God's grand, limitless imagination spills into everything. He is Creator God.

MARCH 12

God puts each morning, each new chance of life, into our hands as a gift to see what we will do with it.

Just as there comes a warm sunbeam into every cottage window, so comes a love—born of God's care for every separate need.

NATHANIEL HAWTHORNE

Taken separately, the experiences of life can work harm and not good. Taken together, they make a pattern of blessing and strength the like of which the world does not know.

V. RAYMOND EDMAN

OCTOBER 23

One of the most wonderful things about knowing God is that there's always so much more to know, so much more to discover.

JONI EARECKSON TADA

Ask, and you will be given what you ask for. Seek, and you will find. Knock, and the door will be opened. For everyone who asks, receives. Anyone who seeks, finds. If only you will knock, the door will open.

MATTHEW 7:7,8 TLB

His joy is in those who reverence him, those who expect him to be loving and kind.

PSALM 147:11   TLB

Love is the reason behind everything God does.

OCTOBER 25

God passes through the thicket of the world, and wherever His glance falls He turns all things to beauty.

JOHN OF THE CROSS

Compassion for others comes when we see ourselves as God sees us.

JANETTE OKE

OCTOBER 26

*Real happiness is not
dependent on external things....
The kind of happiness that
stays with you is the happiness
that springs from inward
thoughts and emotions.*

LILLIAN EICHLER WATSON

MARCH 7

*Happiness held
is the seed.
Happiness shared
is the flower.*

If it's nothing more than a smile—give that away and keep on giving it.

BETH BROWN

MARCH 6

Though our feelings come and go, God's love for us does not.

C. S. LEWIS

OCTOBER 28

Friendship, like the immortality of the soul, is too good to be believed. When friendships are real, they are not glass threads or frost work, but the solidest things we know.

RALPH WALDO EMERSON

MARCH 5

The Lord is fair in everything he does, and full of kindness. He is close to all who call on him sincerely. He fulfills the desires of those who reverence and trust him.

PSALM 145:17-19 TLB

OCTOBER 29

Let the beloved of the Lord rest secure in him, for he shields him all day long, and the one the Lord loves rests between his shoulders.

DEUTERONOMY 33:12 NIV

Joy is warm and radiant and clamors for expressions and experience.

DOROTHY SEGOVIA

God loves and cares for us, even to the least event and smallest need of life.

HENRY EDWARD MANNING

We all mold one another's dreams. We all hold each other's fragile hope in our hands. We all touch others' hearts.

May happiness touch your life today as warmly as you have touched the lives of others.

Look for the heaven here on earth. It is all around you.

NOVEMBER 1

What we do is less than a drop in the ocean. But if that drop were missing, the ocean would lack something.

MOTHER TERESA

MARCH 1

He will yet fill your mouth with laughter and your lips with shouts of joy.

JOB 8:21 NIV

The secret of life is that all we have and are is a gift of grace to be shared.

LLOYD JOHN OGILVIE

FEBRUARY 29

God doesn't always give us explanations, but He did give us His only Son.

NOVEMBER 3

May the Lord of peace himself give you peace at all times and in every way.

2 THESSALONIANS 3:16 NIV

The real joy of life is in its play. Play is anything we do for the joy and love of doing it.... It is the real living of life.

WALTER RAUSCHENBUSCH

NOVEMBER 4

God is constantly taking knowledge of me in love, and watching over me for my good.

J. I. PACKER

Love is an act of endless forgiveness, a tender look which becomes a habit.

PETER USTINOV

NOVEMBER 5

We need to recapture the power of imagination; we shall find that life can be full of wonder, mystery, beauty, and joy.

HAROLD SPENCER JONES

FEBRUARY 26

My Presence will go with you, and I will give you rest.

EXODUS 33:14   NIV

NOVEMBER 6

God is every moment
totally aware of each one
of us. Totally aware in intense
concentration and love.... No
one passes through any area
of life, happy or tragic, without
the attention of God.

EUGENIA PRICE

Joys come from simple and natural things: mists over meadows, sunlight on leaves, the path of the moon over water.

SIGURD F. OLSON

If nothing seems to go my way today, this is my happiness: God is my Father and I am His child.

BASILEA SCHLINK

FEBRUARY 24

Oh, the miraculous energy that flows between two people who care enough…to take the risks of…responding with the whole heart.

ALEX NOBLE

NOVEMBER 8

Show me the wonder of your great love.... Keep me as the apple of your eye; hide me in the shadow of your wings.

PSALM 17:7,8 NIV

A joyful heart is life itself, and rejoicing lengthens one's life.

ECCLESIASTICUS

*This love of God
is nothing less than
the life of God poured
out lavishly and
constantly.*

W. PHILLIP KELLER

It is a fine seasoning for joy to think of those we love.

MOLIÉRE

The fruit of our placing all things in His hands is the presence of His abiding peace in our hearts.

HANNAH WHITALL SMITH

Let him have all your worries and cares, for he is always thinking about you and watching everything that concerns you.

1 PETER 5:7 TLB

One today is worth two tomorrows.

BENJAMIN FRANKLIN

The three grand essentials of happiness are: something to do, something to love, and something to hope for.

THOMAS CHALMERS

NOVEMBER 12

Let us believe that God is in all our simplest deeds and learn to find Him there.

A.W. TOZER

FEBRUARY 19

A thing of beauty is a joy for ever: Its loveliness increases; it will never pass into nothingness.

JOHN KEATS

NOVEMBER 13

Two are better than one.... For if they fall, one will lift up the other.

ECCLESIASTES 4:9,10   NRSV

God's fingers can touch nothing but to mold it into loveliness.

GEORGE MACDONALD

God is not too great to be concerned about our smallest wishes.

BASILEA SCHLINK

He himself gives life and breath to everything, and satisfies every need there is.

ACTS 17:25 TLB

NOVEMBER 15

The highest love of all finds its fulfillment not in what it keeps, but in what it gives.

FATHER ANDREW SDC

Happiness always looks small while you hold it in your hands, but let it go, and you learn at once how big and precious it is.

MAKSIM GORKY

NOVEMBER 16

I wish you sunshine on your path and storms to season your journey. I wish you peace—in the world in which you live and in the smallest corner of the heart where truth is kept.

ROBERT A. WARD

To understand and to be understood makes our happiness on earth.

GERMAN PROVERB

NOVEMBER 17

Happiness itself is a kind of gratitude.

JOSEPH W. KRUTCH

FEBRUARY 14

Something that is stronger and deeper than any words is found in love.

O Lord, deal with me as your child, as one who bears your name!

PSALM 109:21 TLB

FEBRUARY 13

We know that in all things God works for the good of those who love him.

ROMANS 8:28   NIV

NOVEMBER 19

[God's] love for me
is ever the same. It is
the one constant left
in life today.

ALICE CHAPIN

FEBRUARY 12

In the eyes of the King, you have value simply because you are. You don't have to look nice or perform well. Your value is inborn.

MAX LUCADO

With kindness, the difficult becomes easy, the obscure clear; life assumes a charm and its miseries are softened.

CHARLES WAGNER

To be able to find joy in another's joy, that is the secret of happiness.

GEORGE BERNANOS

NOVEMBER 21

Hands down, Thanksgiving is my favorite holiday. It highlights the home and family. It is synonymous with stuff that can be found only at home.

CHARLES R. SWINDOLL

Where the soul is full of peace and joy, outward surroundings and circumstances are of comparatively little account.

HANNAH WHITALL SMITH

NOVEMBER 22

*God is the God of promise.
He keeps His word, even
when that seems impossible;
even when the circumstances
seem to point to the opposite.*

COLIN URQUHART

You're blessed when you're at the end of your rope. With less of you there is more of God and his rule.

MATTHEW 5:3 TM

NOVEMBER 23

In every thing give thanks.

1 THESSALONIANS 5:18 KJV

There is nothing but God's grace. We walk upon it; we breathe it; we live and die by it.

ROBERT LOUIS STEVENSON

NOVEMBER 24

Never lose an opportunity of seeing anything that is beautiful; for beauty is God's handwriting.... Thank God for it.

RALPH WALDO EMERSON

Your greatest pleasure is that which rebounds from hearts you have made glad.

HENRY WARD BEECHER

NOVEMBER 25

Thanksgiving is a time of quiet reflection upon the past and an annual reminder that God has, again, been ever so faithful. The solid and simple things of life are brought into clear focus.

CHARLES R. SWINDOLL

FEBRUARY 6

*A true friend is
one who is concerned
about what we are
becoming, who sees beyond
the present relationship, and
cares deeply about us as
a whole person.*

GLORIA GAITHER

That we are alive
today is proof positive
that God has something
for us to do today.

ANNA R. B. LINDSAY

FEBRUARY 5

When we allow God the privilege of shaping our lives, we discover new depths of purpose and meaning.

JONI EARECKSON TADA

NOVEMBER 27

There is always something for which to be thankful.

CHARLES DICKENS

FEBRUARY 4

They that wait upon the Lord shall renew their strength; They shall mount up with wings as eagles; they shall run, and not be weary; and they shall walk, and not faint.

ISAIAH 40:31 KJV

NOVEMBER 28

Gratitude. More aware of what you have than what you don't. Recognizing the treasure in the simple.... Relishing in the comfort of the common.

MAX LUCADO

FEBRUARY 3

Love, consolation, and peace bloom only in the garden of sweet contentment.

MARTHA ANDERSON

NOVEMBER 29

*Thanks are
the highest form
of thought, and that
gratitude is happiness
doubled by wonder.*

G. K. CHESTERTON

FEBRUARY 2

I asked God for all things that I might enjoy life. He gave me life that I might enjoy all things.

NOVEMBER 30

Commit your way to the Lord; trust in him and he will do this: He will make your righteousness shine like the dawn.

PSALM 37:5 NIV

FEBRUARY 1

Yesterday is already a dream and tomorrow is only a vision. But today well lived makes every yesterday a dream of happiness and every tomorrow a vision of hope.

DECEMBER 1

Beauty is simply reality seen with the eyes of love.

EVELYN UNDERHILL

Contentment is not the fulfillment of what you want, but the realization of how much you already have.

Faith is what makes life bearable, with all its tragedies and ambiguities and sudden, startling joys.

MADELEINE L'ENGLE

JANUARY 30

Our steps are made firm by the Lord, when he delights in our way; though we stumble, we shall not fall headlong, for the Lord holds us by the hand.

PSALM 37:23,24   NRSV

How very much our heavenly Father loves us, for he allows us to be called his children.

1 JOHN 3:1 TLB

Into all our lives, in many simple, familiar ways, God infuses an element of joy from the surprises of life, which unexpectedly brighten our days.

SAMUEL LONGFELLOW

DECEMBER 4

Kind words can be short and easy to speak, but their echoes are truly endless.

MOTHER TERESA

God wants a
relationship with us...
He patiently waits
for us to allow Him
fully into our lives.

CECE WINANS

May you grow to
be as beautiful as God
meant you to be when
He first thought of you.

Friends...they cherish one another's hopes. They are kind to one another's dreams.

HENRY DAVID THOREAU

I have a heart with room for every joy.

P. J. BAILEY

JANUARY 26

You made my whole being, you formed me in my mother's body. I praise you because you made me in an amazing and wonderful way.... All the days planned for me were written in your book before I was one day old.

PSALM 139:13,16 NCV

A grateful heart is the mainspring of happiness.

OSSIAN LAND

The happiness of life is made up of little things — a smile, a hug, a moment of shared laughter.

DECEMBER 8

It is God...who made the garden grow in your hearts.

1 CORINTHIANS 3:6 TLB

God takes life's pieces and gives us unbroken peace.

GOUGH

DECEMBER 9

Time is a very precious gift of God; so precious that it's only given to us moment by moment.

AMELIA BARR

JANUARY 23

The Lord cares intimately for you, knowing you by name. Present yourself to Him. Listen for Him, to Him. He is the Good Shepherd; you can trust Him.

NANCIE CARMICHAEL

Live each moment and be grateful for what it brings, asking no more.

GLORIA GAITHER

That I am here is a wonderful mystery to which I will respond with joy.

*A little nonsense
now and then is
relished by the
wisest men.*

JANUARY 21

A smile takes but a moment, but its effects sometimes last forever.

J. E. SMITH

Faith expects from God what is beyond all expectation.

ANDREW MURRAY

JANUARY 20

Lord...keep me as the apple of Your eye, hide me under the shadow of Your wings.

PSALM 17:1,8 NKJV

Look to the Lord and his strength; seek his face always. Remember the wonders he has done.

PSALM 105:4,5 NIV

JANUARY 19

Life is so full of meaning and purpose, so full of beauty — beneath its covering — that you will find that earth but cloaks your heaven.

FRA GIOVANNI

DECEMBER 14

*When one helps
another, both
are strong.*

GERMAN PROVERB

JANUARY 18

God has put something noble and good into every heart His hand created.

MARK TWAIN

DECEMBER 15

The heart of the giver makes the gift dear and precious.

MARTIN LUTHER

JANUARY 17

Remember you are very special to God as His precious child. He has promised to complete the good work He has begun in you. As you continue to grow in Him, He will teach you to be a blessing to others.

GARY SMALLEY & JOHN TRENT

DECEMBER 16

Again Christmas: abiding point of return. Set apart by its mystery, mood, and magic, the season seems in a way to stand outside time. All that is dear, that is lasting, renews its hold on us: we are home again.

ELIZABETH BOWEN

What do we live for,
if not to make the
world less difficult
for each other?

GEORGE ELIOT

DECEMBER 17

Recall it as often as you wish, a happy memory never wears out.

LIBBIE FUDIM

Something deep in all of us yearns for God's beauty, and we can find it no matter where we are.

SUE MONK KIDD

DECEMBER 18

The most vivid memories of Christmases past are usually not of gifts given or received, but of the spirit of love, the special warmth of Christmas worship, the cherished little habits of the home.

LOIS RAND

How great is the love the Father has lavished on us, that we should be called the children of God! And that is what we are!

1 JOHN 3:1 NIV

DECEMBER 19

Behold, a virgin shall be with child, and shall bring forth a son, and they shall call his name Emmanuel... God with us.

MATTHEW 1:23 KJV

JANUARY 13

We do not understand the intricate pattern of the stars in their course, but we know that He who created them does, and that just as surely as He guides them, He is charting a safe course for us.

BILLY GRAHAM

Christmas, my child, is love in action.... When you love someone, you give to them, as God gives to us. The greatest gift He ever gave was the person of His Son, sent to us in human form.

DALE EVANS ROGERS

Joy comes from within.

*Oh, come to us,
abide with us, our
Lord Emmanuel!*

PHILLIPS BROOKS

JANUARY 11

The glory is not in never failing, but in rising every time you fail.

CHINESE PROVERB

DECEMBER 22

Let this Christmas season be a renewing of the mind of Christ in our thinking, and a cleansing of our lives by His pure presence. Let His joy come to our weary world through us.

GERALD KENNEDY

Everyone has inside himself a piece of good news! The good news is that you really don't know how great you can be, how much you can love, what you can accomplish, and what your potential is.

ANNE FRANK

DECEMBER 23

Christmas is the celebration of the keeping of a promise... the promise that He would someday walk with us, that we might be His people and He our God.... A saving promise.

MICHAEL CARD

JANUARY 9

God surrounds [us] with his loving care.

DEUTERONOMY 33:12   TLB

DECEMBER 24

God grant you the light in Christmas, which is faith; the warmth of Christmas, which is love...the belief in Christmas, which is truth; the all of Christmas, which is Christ.

WILDA ENGLISH

JANUARY 8

*You are in the Beloved...
therefore infinitely dear to
the Father, unspeakably
precious to Him. You
are never, not for one
second, alone.*

NORMAN F. DOWTY

DECEMBER 25

*For unto us a Child is born,
Unto us a Son is given;
And the government will
be upon His shoulder.
And His name will be called
Wonderful, Counselor, Mighty
God, Everlasting Father,
Prince of Peace.*

ISAIAH 9:6 NKJV

JANUARY 7

Our joy will be complete if we remain in His love — for His love is personal, intimate, real, living, delicate, faithful love.

MOTHER TERESA

True worth is in being,
not seeming—
In doing, each day that
goes by,
Some little good—not
in dreaming
Of great things to do by
and by.

ALICE CARY

Those who run in the path of God's commands have their hearts set free.

Our Creator would never have made such lovely days and have given us the deep hearts to enjoy them, above and beyond all thought, unless we were meant to be immortal.

NATHANIEL HAWTHORNE

Every day under the sun is a gift. Receive it with eagerness. Treat it kindly. Share it with joy. Each night return it to the Giver who will make it bright and shiny again before the next sunrise.

DECEMBER 28

*Blessings brighten
when we count them.*

MALTBIE D. BABCOCK

How precious it is, Lord, to realize that you are thinking about me constantly! I can't even count how many times a day your thoughts turn towards me.

PSALM 139:17 TLB

DECEMBER 29

*Thanks be
to God for his
indescribable gift!*

2 CORINTHIANS 9:15 NIV

JANUARY 3

Every day in a life fills the whole life with expectation and memories.

C. S. LEWIS

DECEMBER 30

If we celebrate the years behind us they become stepping stones of strength and joy for the years ahead.

JANUARY 2

God is the beginning — not just the starting point, but the source of all things.

MARILYN M. MORGAN

DECEMBER 31

It is God to whom and with whom we travel, and while He is the end of our journey, He is also at every stopping place.

ELISABETH ELLIOT

JANUARY 1

*There is always
a time for gratitude
and new beginnings.*

ROBERT MOSKIN